# THE RELIEF OF BELSEN, APRIL 1945

## EYEWITNESS ACCOUNTS

IMPERIAL WAR

MUSEUM

Published by the Imperial War Museum,
Lambeth Road, London SE1 6HZ

© Trustees of the Imperial War Museum, 1991

Compiled by Paul Kemp, Department of Photographs, Imperial War Museum

Designed by Tina Ranft

Printed in England by George Over Limited, Rugby


British Library Cataloguing-in-Publication Data
A catalogue record for this book is available from the British Library
ISBN 0 901627 70 4

Front cover: A British soldier talks to an inmate of Belsen shortly after the liberation of the camp, 17 April 1945. BU 4002

Back cover: A former inmate weeps over one of the mass graves at Belsen, 14 August 1946. BU 12578

# FOREWORD

This booklet stems from a permanent exhibition on the relief of the camp at Bergen-Belsen, which was opened in the Imperial War Museum in 1991. These facts are unremarkable in themselves, but they disguise much about both the Museum and its public. During the 1980s the Imperial War Museum underwent a radical transformation, embarking upon a grand redevelopment scheme for our Main Building, including entirely new galleries and displays. The first stage of this was completed and opened in 1989. However, it involved more than a physical reconstruction, since there was a growing awareness amongst those who worked in the Museum that public interest in and knowledge of the First and Second World Wars was changing. In part this was because the people who experienced these wars directly now formed a decreasing minority of visitors, the majority of whom were born into a world of at least nominal peace. It seemed all the more important for us to try and put the World Wars into a context which would have relevance to today's visitors and to make our displays more than a nostalgic journey into a near-forgotten reality.

The impact which the newsreel films of Belsen made at the end of the war was enormous. People saw and understood for the first time the depth of horror to which state and institutional barbarism can lead and many still remember exactly where and when they first saw these awful images. Sadly, however, the post-war world has not been free from such extreme violence and the television news carries pictures of mass graves and mutilated bodies all too often. It was against this historical background that we decided to give special prominence to our holdings on Belsen, both as a record of ultimate depravity and as an extraordinary story of survival and recovery. The relief of Belsen is indeed a tale of and for our century.

It is interesting to note the public reaction to our display. Even the noisiest school party falls silent, people look intently and carefully, and leave the Belsen area in a sober and serious mood. They may think too of the civil wars and regional conflicts of recent years, which produce those television horrors, but somehow the scale, the timeframe, and the deliberate nature of Nazi brutality makes it perennially shocking and disturbing. This is why we should and do display it and why we publish this book. We do not aim just to shock, but to record and to remember, not least the efforts of the medical personnel who saved many thousands of lives in the spring and summer of 1945. Eventually, perhaps, the whole world will learn to live in a truly peaceful and civilised manner, but until it does Belsen is there to warn us of the consequences.

Alan Borg
Director-General, Imperial War Museum

# ACKNOWLEDGMENTS

The Museum wishes to thank the following individuals and institutions for allowing their material to be used in this book: BBC Sound Archives for use of Richard Dimbleby's broadcast; David Bradford; Michael Coigley; Brigadier Robert Daniell; John Dixey; Zdenka Ehrlich; Kathleen Elvidge; Christopher Gonin (for use of extracts from the papers of Lieutenant-Colonel M W Gonin); Andrew Matthews; A Midgley; Ian Proctor; Frederick Riches; Dr Hadassah Rosensaft; Derek Sington; Mrs V Smithman; and Colonel E Vella RAMC.

The Museum also wishes to acknowledge the contribution made by the following to the research for this book: the Controller of HM Stationery Office; the Librarian and staff of the Library, St Thomas's Hospital Medical School, London; Dr Thomas Rahe of the Niedersächsische Landeszentrale für Politische Bildung, Hanover; Dr Ursula Guly; Genya Markon of the United States Holocaust Memorial Museum; Jo Churchill of the Queen Alexandra's Royal Army Nursing Corps Museum, Aldershot; and the Royal Army Medical Corps Historical Museum, Aldershot.

# INTRODUCTION

In the overall context of Hitler's campaign against the Jews the camp at Bergen-Belsen (hereafter referred to as Belsen) occupied a unique place within the concentration camp system. It was not an extermination centre such as Birkenau or Treblinka, nor was it a work camp like Mauthausen or Dachau. Belsen, near Hanover in north-west Germany, was established as a special camp for prominent Jews who were either citizens of neutral states or who were seen as useful hostages for the Reich or alternatively as a means of exchange for German citizens interned abroad. Conditions in the camp were initially quite good, by concentration camp standards, but from 1944 they deteriorated rapidly. In March 1944 the camp was euphemistically redesignated a 'Recovery Camp' [*Ehrholungslager*] for prisoners from other camps who were considered too ill to work. As the German army was forced onto the defensive by the twin onslaughts of the British and American forces in the west and the Red Army in the east, so the concentration camps in the path of these advancing allied armies were cleared and their exhausted, sick and dying inhabitants sent to Belsen. The facilities in Belsen were totally unable to cope with this influx and basic services – food, water and sanitation – swiftly collapsed. In these conditions diseases such as typhus, dysentery and tuberculosis flourished and quickly reached epidemic proportions. By April 1945 there were over 60,000 prisoners in Belsen living in the most appalling conditions. The horrifying scenes found by the British Army when they liberated the camp on 15 April 1945 have come to symbolise the worst excesses and inhuman barbarity of the Nazi regime.

## The history of Belsen, 1943–45: a chronology

**March 1943**

Heinrich Himmler, leader of the SS and responsible for the concentration camps, had earlier ordered the establishment of a special camp for prominent European Jews or Jewish citizens of neutral states, known as 'Exchange' Jews, who could be exchanged for German citizens interned abroad. Himmler directed that although the inmates of the camp were to work they were to be well treated. SS Hauptsturmführer Adolf Haas is appointed Kommandant.

**July 1943**

Stalag 311, a PoW camp near the village of Belsen is selected as the site for the camp and the first transports of prisoners arrive. By August 1944 there are thousands of 'Exchange' Jews in Belsen housed in different sections of the camp according to their status:

*Neutralenlager* (Neutrals' Camp) holds 300 Jews who are citizens of neutral states. Food and sanitation in this area of the camp are of a reasonable standard and the prisoners do not have to work.

*Sonderlager* (Special Camp) houses 350 Jews of Polish origin who are citizens of neutral states or who possess Palestine emigration papers. Their segregation from the other 'Exchange' Jews is to prevent their telling of the massacres and the deliberate extermination of European Jewry they will have witnessed in Poland.

*Ungarnlager* (Hungarians' Camp) is opened in July 1944 for 1,683 Hungarian Jews due to be sent to Switzerland. Conditions are good and the inmates do not have to work.

*Sternlager* (Star Camp), so called because of the Star of David worn by the prisoners on their clothes. This section holds the 3,000 'Exchange' Jews proper who have to work although they are allowed a limited amount of self-government with a Jewish Council, *Judenrat*, to administer the camp.

*Haftlingslager* (Prisoners' Camp) contains the 500 prisoners from Buchenwald and Natzweiler who built the camp. The prisoners are employed on hard labour and are brutally treated by the SS guards.

**March 1944**

Belsen is redesignated an *Ehrholungslager* (Recovery Camp) for prisoners from other concentration camps considered too weak to work. No additional medical facilities are provided so that a prisoner sent to Belsen for recovery is in fact being condemned to death by neglect, disease and starvation.

**July 1944**

A *Frauenlager* (Women's Camp) is established for women and girls evacuated from camps in the east in the face of the advancing Red Army. By December 1944 8,000 women and girls are housed in conditions of extreme squalor in hastily-built barracks.

**2 December 1944**

SS Hauptsturmführer Josef Kramer replaces Haas as Kommandant, an experienced concentration camp officer who feels no compassion for the prisoners in his charge. One of his first decisions is to end the privileged regime enjoyed by inmates in the *Sternlager* although he makes no change to the status of those in the *Neutralenlager* or *Sonderlager*.

An official census shows that there are 15,257 prisoners in the camp.

A man, dying of starvation, sits by one of the fences separating the various sections of the camp. BU 3728

| January 1945 | The number of prisoners in the camp continues to increase as thousands of prisoners evacuated from camps in Eastern Europe are sent to Belsen. |
| --- | --- |
| | To accommodate the additional prisoners, the SS take over the remaining portion of Stalag 311 which becomes the new *Frauenlager*. The old *Frauenlager* is turned into a second prisoners' camp and named *Haftlingslager II*. Despite the expansion of the camp there is still insufficient room for all the inmates. |
| February 1945 | The approximate population in the camp is 22,000 men and women, of whom 7,000 die during the month. |
| | The prisoners, many of whom are seriously ill, are packed into already overcrowded barracks or speedily-erected huts. Typhus makes its first appearance and begins to spread through the camp. Other diseases, chiefly tuberculosis and dysentery, are also widespread. |
| March 1945 | The numbers in the camp have risen to 41,520 men and women, 18,168 of whom die during the month. |
| | The prisoners begin to starve as the food supply breaks down. The daily ration consists of a bowl of thin soup. Despite the ready availability of food in the neighbourhood the SS make no attempt to procure additional supplies. There is evidence of cannibalism in the camp. |
| 4 March 1945 | Operations begin to clear the inmates of the *Neutralenlager*, *Sonderlager* and *Sternlager*. 105 Turkish citizens leave the *Neutralenlager* for Sweden. |
| 1 April 1945 | There are an estimated 44,000 men and women in the camp. In the two weeks up to 15 April approximately 9,000 prisoners die of disease and starvation. With no facilities for their disposal a large number of corpses are simply left lying all over the camp. |
| | The sanitary system, which has never been designed to supply the needs of so many, breaks down. With most of the inmates suffering from chronic diarrhoea the vicious circle of disease, exacerbated by lack of decent sanitation, leading to further outbreaks of disease, is complete. |
| 8 April 1945 | Further transports containing 25,000–30,000 prisoners from other concentration camps in the Neuengamme area arrive at Belsen bringing the number of inmates to over 60,000. There is no room for them all, so some are housed in the nearby army barracks. |
| 11 April 1945 | Three transports containing the 7,000 remaining inmates from the *Neutralenlager*, *Sonderlager* and *Sternlager* leave the camp for Switzerland. One transport reaches Theresienstadt while the other two are liberated by the Allied armies. The departure of these transports marks the end of Belsen's role as a special camp. |
| | The sound of the advancing British forces is now clearly audible. The SS guards attempt to conceal the 10,000 unburied corpses. |
| | A detachment from GHQ Liaison Regiment 'Phantom', probing ahead of the advancing British forces, passes the camp. |
| 12 April 1945 | As British forces approach Celle the local German Army commander requests that a neutral area be established around the concentration camp at Belsen. The agreement is concluded on 12 April and provides for a forty-eight square kilometre zone around the camp into which only medical units associated with relief work will be allowed to enter. At this stage there is no indication of the true state of affairs at Belsen. At some time between 12 and 15 April, Lieutenant-Colonel Robert Daniell, commanding officer of 13 Regiment, Honourable Artillery Company, Royal Horse Artillery, is the first British soldier to enter the camp. However, because his unit is in contact with the retreating Germans, he is unable to do anything other than note the horrific conditions. |
| 15 April 1945 | The first units of the British Army arrive. Kramer is placed under arrest. |

# THE RELIEF OF THE CAMP

The relief operation which followed the liberation of the camp was largely directed by Brigadier H L Glyn-Hughes, Deputy Director of Medical Services (DDMS) Second Army. It was improvised at great speed and relied much on the initiative and resourcefulness of those involved. Within a few weeks of liberation and with very limited means, the Royal Army Medical Corps and other units had transformed the situation in the camp. The inmates were moved into hastily-established hospitals or better accommodation, food supplies and clean water were organised, schools were set up and the dead buried. Much of this took place before the German capitulation and with the front line only a few miles away.

**15 April**
The first British forces arrive at the camp: a loudspeaker lorry from 14 Amplifier Unit of the Intelligence Corps followed by 63 Anti-Tank Regiment, Royal Artillery.

Brigadier Llewelyn Glyn-Hughes, DDMS Second Army, visits the camp and takes control of the relief operation. It becomes clear that the situation is beyond the resources of 63 AT Regiment to deal with, so units of the Royal Army Medical Corps (RAMC) are ordered to the camp. An appeal is also made to the Red Cross and UNRRA (United Nations Relief and Rehabilitation Association).

**17 April**
Units of the RAMC arrive. A conference of the medical officers decides that it is essential to evacuate the camp and create a vast hospital area in the nearby German army barracks. 11 Light Field Ambulance are to move the inmates out of the camp into the hospitals to be established by 32 Casualty Clearing Station. Typhus control in Belsen and the surrounding area is made the responsibility of 30 Field Hygiene Section.

**18 April**
No.10 Garrison Detachment assume responsibility for running the camp. 113 Light Anti-Aircraft Regiment, Royal Artillery relieve 63 Anti-Tank Regiment for general duties in the camp.

The burial of the dead. At first the SS guards are made to collect the bodies and bury them. Eventually a bulldozer has to be used to push bodies into the mass graves. Services are read over the graves by army rabbis and chaplains.

A Jewish Camp Committee is set up by former inmates under the chairmanship of Josef Rosensaft.

**20 April**
Evacuation of the camp has to be postponed for twenty four hours after the Germans, clearing their barracks under the terms of the truce, deliberately sabotage the water supply.

1575 Platoon, Royal Army Service Corps take over the administration and distribution of food supplies.

**21 April**
Evacuation of the camp begins. All inmates are to be moved, after being deloused, into the newly-established hospitals or clean barrack accommodation. While the evacuation is in progress, efforts are made to improve conditions for the thousands forced to remain until space becomes available in the hospitals. As each hut is cleared it is burned.

From 21 April until 9 May 1,100 people are evacuated each day.

**23 April**
Arrival of six detachments of the British Red Cross.

**25 April**
The daily death rate in the camp from disease and starvation is estimated at between four and five hundred people.

**28 April**
The burial of the dead is complete.

**29 April**
The SS guards employed in collecting corpses for burial are transferred to prison at Celle.

**30 April**
Ninety seven medical students from London teaching hospitals arrive to assist in the relief operation.

**4 May**
Further units of the Royal Army Medical Corps arrive: Nos 9 and 29 General Hospitals; 163 Field Ambulance; 35 Casualty Clearing Station and 76 Field Hygiene Section.

| | |
|---|---|
| **8 May** | VE Day: hostilities in Europe cease. |
| **11 May** | The death rate among the former inmates falls to below 100 per day. |
| **19 May** | Evacuation of the camp is complete. All the former inmates are now housed in the nearby barracks or hospitals while arrangements are made for their repatriation. |
| **21 May** | The ceremonial burning of the last hut brings to an end the first stage of the relief operation. |
| **28 May** | The British medical students return to London. Their place is taken by volunteers from Belgian hospitals. |
| **July** | Six thousand former inmates are taken by the Red Cross to Sweden for convalescence. |
| | UNRRA officials begin the task of arranging repatriation. |
| **17 September** | The trial opens at Luneburg before a British Military Court of forty five former guards at Belsen including Josef Kramer, commandant; Fritz Klein, camp doctor; Elisabeth Volkenrath, head wardress and Irma Grese – a wardress renowned for her cruelty. |
| **17 November** | Kramer and ten others are sentenced to death. Twenty of the other accused are sentenced to terms of imprisonment and the remaining fourteen are acquitted. |
| **June 1945** | Belsen becomes a Displaced Persons' camp with a largely Jewish population who have to wait there until their emigration to Palestine can be arranged. During this period Belsen becomes a self-governing Jewish enclave in the British Zone of occupied Germany with a flourishing cultural life. |
| **6 September 1950** | The last former inmate leaves Belsen for Palestine and the camp is finally closed. |

# LIBERATION

British forces of 11 Armoured Division discovered the concentration camp at Bergen-Belsen almost by accident in April 1945 during their advance through north-west Germany. The first British troops to arrive could only note the conditions with disbelief before they continued their pursuit of the retreating Wehrmacht. An agreement was later concluded on 12 April between VIII Corps and the local German commander for the area around the camp to be declared a neutral zone. On 15 April leading elements of 63 Anti-Tank Regiment, Royal Artillery assumed control of the camp. It rapidly became clear that local resources could not deal with the situation so an appeal was made for additional medical and supporting units, the first of which arrived on 17 April.

About 10am one brilliantly fine morning in April 1945, Brigadier Roscoe Harvey, commanding 29 Armoured Brigade, and myself, with a few tanks, arrived at the entrance of what appeared to be a small heavily wired-in camp. With all the regiments of the Armoured Brigade in fierce contact with the enemy, Roscoe wisely stayed out of the camp but he asked me to go in and report on what I found.

Firstly I went over to have a look at a few cattle trucks on a siding near by. Finding them still containing 20 or 30 dead men and women, the nature of this camp hidden away in the woods was immediately apparent.

Inside (*one of the huts*) a sight revealed itself that daunted even a battle-experienced man like myself. Inside there were tiers of bunks containing one and sometimes even three completely naked human beings, the stench was appalling. It was a truly terrible sight, quite obviously they had received no food or medical attention for some time, yet outside were lusty young SS soldiers, fit and well, milling around.

I had had enough. Never will I forget what I had seen that

day and never will I forgive the race who produced men capable of (*causing*) such cold blooded misery and death to the thousands who were driven into Belsen Camp.

*Brigadier R B T Daniell DSO, Commanding Officer 13 Regiment, Honourable Artillery Company, Royal Horse Artillery*

On 13 April I received written instructions from BGS VIII Corps that I was to assume control of the area as given in the agreement, that I was to command all enemy troops remaining in the area.

Early on 14 April I joined the Battery in 11 Armoured Division area near Issel but it was not until approximately midday on 15 April that our forward troops penetrated the area which was to be regarded as neutral.

At 1330 hours a Liaison Officer, Captain P T Ashton, was sent immediately behind 23rd Hussars to contact (*the local German Army commander*) Oberst Harries, and to arrange for the latter to meet me at the entrance to the camp. Upon contacting Oberst Harries I explained to him, through an interpreter, that I was the Allied Military Commander and demanded to be shown quarters for my troops. I had previously arranged that a loudspeaker van should broadcast a message from the Corps Commander as soon as it was possible to enter the camp.

*Lieutenant-Colonel R I G Taylor DSO MC, Commanding Officer 63 Anti-Tank Regiment, Royal Artillery*

In the night before April 15 I lay awake and only fell asleep in the small hours. Suddenly I was woken up by one of the Russian workers in our block. 'Come, come quick! Quick! There are tanks on the street!' I heard the unmistakable clanking, rumbling noise . . . From far I heard the tanks pass through the camp entrance and a voice call from a loud speaker van. I knew we were free.

*Rudolf Kustermeier, inmate*

Death rate 17,000 in March. Thousands of corpses lying unburied. Inmates starving to death every day. Water and food finished. No light or sanitation. Hundreds dying.

*Brigadier J Melvin, Deputy-Director of Medical Services VIII Corps*

**Aerial reconnaissance photograph of Belsen concentration camp taken on 19 September 1944 by the Royal Air Force. Air Photo Library, University of Keele.**

**Blindfolded German officers leaving the HQ of VIII Corps during the negotiations for the handover of the camp, 12/13 April 1945. BU 3624**

I received a signal that at the special request of the DDMS 2nd Army the unit was required to move to Belsen. Special requests are not usually made at Army level so, realising the honour, we 'up sticks' and moved. I knew no more than someone had found a concentration camp and that they thought there was typhus in it.

*Lieutenant-Colonel M W Gonin, Commanding Officer 11 Light Field Ambulance, Royal Army Medical Corps*

We was about five miles from the camp. We didn't know nothing about Belsen at all. The next morning we was told to assemble ourselves on the road with all vehicles and everything else and we was moved down the road and we passed Belsen on the way to the next field where we was going to stop. Even then we didn't know that it was a concentration camp or anything like that. All we could smell was the atmosphere itself and it was really horrible. Then an officer come out, he says, 'What you passed just now is a concentration camp.'

*Private Frederick Riches, ambulance driver, 11 Light Field Ambulance, Royal Army Medical Corps*

As we walked down the main roadway of the camp we were cheered by the internees and for the first time we saw their condition.

A great number of them were little more than living skeletons with haggard yellowish faces. Most of the men wore a striped pyjama type of clothing – others wore rags, while women wore striped flannel gowns or any other clothing they had managed to acquire. Many of them were without shoes and wore only socks and stockings. There were men and women lying in heaps on both sides of the track. Others were walking slowly and aimlessly about – a vacant expression on their starved faces.

I later ordered Kramer to be placed under close arrest and confined to his own sitting room. I then dispatched a Liaison Officer to Corps HQ with an urgent request for food and water and further military aid.

*Lieutenant-Colonel R I G Taylor, Commanding Officer 63 Anti-Tank Regiment, Royal Artillery*

I had tried to visualise the interior of a concentration camp, but I had not imagined it like this. Nor had I imagined the strange simian throng who crowded to the barbed wire fences surrounding the compounds, with their shaven heads and their obscene penitentiary suits, which were so dehumanising.

We had experienced gratitude and welcome in France, Belgium and Holland. We had been surrounded in Paris, embraced and thanked. In Flemish villages our truck had been loaded with tomatoes and ripe pears and jugs of cool beer had been handed to us by local people.

But the half-credulous cheers of these almost lost men, of these clowns in their terrible motley, who had once been Polish officers, land-workers in the Ukraine, Budapest doctors and students in France impelled a stronger emotion and I had to fight back my tears.

*Lieutenant Derek Sington, 14 Amplifier Unit, Intelligence Corps*

# THE SCENE INSIDE THE CAMP

The soldiers and relief workers were totally unprepared for what they found at Belsen and their inability to accept what was happening around them is very apparent in their letters and diaries. Only the medical personnel seemed able to bring a degree of detachment to their descriptions of conditions in the camp.

I have just returned from the Belsen concentration camp where for two hours I drove slowly about the place in a jeep with the chief doctor of Second Army. I had waited a day before going to the camp so I could be absolutely sure of the facts available. I find it hard to describe adequately the horrible things I have seen and heard, but here, unadorned, are the facts.

There are forty thousand men, women and children in the camp. German and half a dozen other nationalities, thousands of them Jews. Of this total of 40,000, 4,250 are acutely ill or are dying of virulent disease. Typhus, typhoid, diphtheria, dysentery, pneumonia, and childbirth fever are rife. 25,600, three quarters of them women, are either ill through lack of food or are actually dying of starvation. In the last few months alone, 30,000 prisoners have been killed off or allowed to die.

Those are the simple, horrible facts of Belsen. But horrible as they are, they can convey little or nothing in themselves. I wish with all my heart that everyone fighting in this war, and above all those whose duty it is to direct the war from Britain and America, could have come with me through the barbed-wire fence that leads to the inner compound of the camp. Outside, it had been the lucky prisoners, the men and women who had only just arrived at Belsen before we captured it. But beyond the barrier was a whirling cloud of dust. The dust of thousands of slowly moving people, laden in itself with the deadly typhus germ. And with the dust was the smell, sickly and thick, the smell of death and decay, of corruption and filth. I passed through the barrier and found myself in a nightmare. Dead bodies, some of them in decay, lay strewn about the road and along the rutted tracks. On each side of the road were brown wooden huts. There were faces at the windows, the bony emaciated faces of starving women, too weak to come outside, propping themselves against the glass to see the daylight before they died. And they were dying, every hour and every minute. I saw a man, wandering dazedly along the road, stagger and fall. Someone else looked down at him, took him by the heels and dragged him to the side of the road to join the other bodies lying unburied there. No-one else took the slightest notice. They didn't even trouble to turn their heads. Behind the huts, two youths and two girls who had found a morsel of food were sitting together on the grass sharing it. They were not six feet from a pile of decomposing bodies.

*Richard Dimbleby, BBC War Correspondent*

**An overall view of the camp taken from one of the perimeter watchtowers. BU 4711**

**The scene in the *Haftlingslager II* section of the camp with the inmates living in makeshift shanties, 17 April 1945. BU 3811**

Today I visited a German concentration camp at Belsen near Celle. I saw some of the most horrible sights imaginable. No words can describe the horror of this place. It must be seen to be believed.

*Sergeant A N Midgley, No. 5 Army Film and Photographic Unit*

I am Vice-Director of Medical Services, British Army of the Rhine and in April of this year was Deputy Director of Medical Services, 2nd Army. Shortly before 15 April of this year, certain German officers came to the Headquarters of V111 Corps and requested a truce in respect of Belsen Camp, which was arranged. On 15 April Lieutenant-Colonel Taylor took over the administration of the camp and I followed him there. When I arrived I found him interrogating Kommandant Kramer, and later on the same evening I saw the medical officer, Dr Klein. I identify these accused. We made a preliminary survey of the camp straight away and on the next day a complete investigation. For the next two or three days I was engaged in organizing relief measures.

Q. I would like to get a general description of the camp.

A. It is situated between the villages of Bergen and Winsen, some 15 miles north of Celle and is quite separate. It consisted of an administrative area nearest the road and beyond that a wired-in perimeter including a large number of huts, chiefly wooden, of various sizes. The camp was divided into five compounds and there was a main road running through the middle.

Q. Did you ask for and receive the number of persons interned in the camp?

A. Yes. Not including Camp 2, there were approximately 41,000 made up of 28,185 women and 12,000 men. There were three compounds for men, one small and one very large compound for women and five cookhouses.

Q. Would you describe the scene in one of the huts as you went into it.

A. There were no bunks in a hut in the Women's Compound which was containing the typhus patients. They were lying on the floor and were so weak they could hardly move. There was practically no bedding. In some cases there was a thin mattress but some had none. Some had no clothing at all and just draped themselves in blankets and some had German hospital type of clothing. That was the general picture.

Q. What was the state of sanitation?

A. There was none. The conditions were indescribable because most of the internees were suffering from some form of gastro-enteritis and they were too weak to leave the hut. The lavatories in the huts had long been out of use. In the Women's Compound there was a deep trench with a pole over it but no screening or form of privacy at all. Those who were strong enough could get into the compound: others performed their natural actions from where they were. The compounds were absolutely one mass of human excreta. In the huts themselves the floors were covered and the people in the top bunks who could not get out just poured it onto the bunks below.

*Cross-examination of Brigadier H L Glyn-Hughes, Vice-Director of Medical Services British Army of the Rhine, by Colonel T M Backhouse, Counsel for the Prosecution, on 18 September 1945 during the Belsen Trial*

Of the inmates of Camp 1 at the time of liberation it was estimated that 5,000 were suffering from famine oedema, 3,500 from typhus, 20,000 from enteritis and 10,000 from tuberculosis. These figures proved, if anything, to be an under-estimation.

*Special Supplement on Belsen published with the* British Zone Review, *13 October 1945*

I can give no adequate description of the Horror Camp in which my men and myself were to spend the next month of our lives. It was just a barren wilderness, as bare and devoid of vegetation as a chicken run. Corpses lay everywhere, some in huge piles where they had been dumped by other inmates, sometimes they lay singly or in pairs where they had fallen as they shuffled along the dirt tracks. Those who died of disease usually died in the huts. When starvation was the chief cause of death they died in the open for it is an odd characteristic of starvation that its victims feel compelled to go on wandering till they fall down and die. Once they had fallen they seem to die almost at once and it took a little time to get used to seeing men, women and children collapse as you walked by them and restrain oneself from going to their assistance. One had to get used early to the idea that the individual just did not count. One knew that 500 a day were dying and 500 a day were going on

**Outside one of the huts women search through the clothing of inmates who have died during the night. BU 3722**

**A British Soldier talks to an inmate of Belsen shortly after the liberation of the camp, 17 April 1945. BU4002**

dying for weeks before anything we could do would have the slightest effect. It was, however, not easy to watch a child choking to death from diphtheria when you knew a tracheotomy and nursing would save it. One saw women drowning in their own vomit because they were too weak to turn over, and men eating worms as they clutched half a loaf of bread purely because they had to eat worms to live and now could scarcely tell the difference between worms and bread.

*Lieutenant-Colonel M W Gonin, Commanding Officer 11 Light Field Ambulance, Royal Army Medical Corps*

The prisoners were a dense mass of emaciated apathetic scarecrows huddled together in wooden huts, and in many cases without beds or blankets, and in some cases without any clothing whatsoever. The females were in worse condition than the men and their clothing generally, if they had any, only filthy rags. The dead lay all over the camp and in piles outside the blocks of huts which housed the worst of the sick and were miscalled hospitals. There were thousands of naked and emaciated corpses in various stages of decomposition lying unburied. Sanitation was to all practical purposes non-existent. Pits with, in only a few instances, wooden perch rails, were available in totally inadequate numbers. The inmates, from starvation, apathy and weakness, defecated and urinated where they sat or lay,

**Interior of one of the women's huts. BU3736**

**A woman crouching on the floor on one of the huts. BU 4863**

14

even inside the living huts. Ablution arrangements were completely inadequate. There was no running water or electricity. All water was brought in by British water trucks.

*Deposition of Lieutenant-Colonel J A D Johnston RAMC, Commanding Officer 32 Casualty Clearing Station, sworn before Major Savile Geoffrey Champion RA, Legal Staff, No. 1 War Crimes Investigation Team*

The problems were:

1. To stop the typhus spreading.

2. To bury the dead before the hot summer started cholera.

3. To feed the sick in the Horror Camp who were dying of starvation more rapidly than of their illness.

4. To remove from the Horror Camp those who might live with some form of systematized feeding and nursing.

5. To help those who lived regain their humanity.

What we had therefore was buildings, 8 nurses, about 300 RAMC chaps, a regiment of LAA, at least 20,000 sick, suffering from the most virulent diseases known to man, all of whom required urgent hospital treatment and 30,000 men, women and children who might not die if they were not doctored but who would most certainly die if they were not fed and removed from the Horror Camp.

What we had not got was nurses, doctors, beds, bedding, clothes, drugs, dressings, thermometers, bedpans or any of the essentials of medical treatment and worst of all no common language.

*Lieutenant-Colonel M W Gonin, Commanding Officer 11 Light Field Ambulance, Royal Army Medical Corps*

In the spring of 1945 I was in my third year at Barts as a clinical student. We were asked if we would be prepared to give up a month of our training to go abroad to do some relief work. Nobody told us exactly what we were going to do, but we thought we were going to Holland to try to do something about the starving children that had been left behind by the Germans after the occupation. And, of course, being medical students, we felt perhaps that we were being rather feather-bedded. Our friends were all in the army, the navy and so on, and had had quite a hectic time. I'd lost several friends who had been at school with me, in the navy and the air force. And this was our chance to get away and to do something, perhaps slightly different, to help the war effort.

*David Bradford, medical student at St Bartholomew's Hospital Medical School*

We go there every day of the week and work from 8.00am until 6.00pm with 1¼ hours break for lunch. I feel dead at the end of it. That is not the end tho' for we have a conference from 6.15 to 7.15 to check upon the chaos here.

**The former camp commandant Josef Kramer, 'The Beast of Belsen', under arrest at Belsen, 17 April 1945. BU 3823**

There is then a council from about 9.30 onwards from Group Leaders and various other officials that have been appointed. We are run by two doctors – one in UNRRA and the other in the RAMC, a veritable firebrand who has worked miracles.

The position as regards us medical students is this. Each one is in charge of a hut and it is his job to see that the inmates are properly fed. For this job we brought over big supplies of glucose vitamin mixture and pre-digested milk protein. I have a Women's hut in which there were 160 people badly ill. Almost all have starvation diarrhoea and are lying huddled almost on top of each other wallowing in filth and crying for attention.

*Letter from Michael Coigley, medical student at St Thomas's Hospital Medical School, 5 May 1945*

We walked into the hut, held our noses, walked round, walked out again, looked at each other and said 'where do we start?'

*Ian Proctor, medical student at St Bartholomew's Hospital Medical School*

I went into the middle of the hut and yelled for someone who could speak English, but got no reply, so I tried in very shaky German. The result was an uproar, but a cleanish looking woman appeared, called Vircha, and said she was in charge of the place. At this point, Whimster turned up with medicine, which consisted of 20 opium tablets .03 gram, 30 aspirins, some tannalbin, which is a German preparation that we had not heard of before, three 3-inch bandages and a packet of gauze.

We took a look round. There was faeces all over the floor,

**British medical students with senior British Army medical officers. Brigadier H L Glyn-Hughes, DDMS Second Army, is seated centre. HU 59497, Andrew Matthews Collection.**

the majority of people having diarrhoea and passing a stool like a small cow pat – there were tin cans and lumps of black bread all mixed up with it, and the place could not have been swept for years. I was standing rather aghast in the middle of all this filth, trying to get used to the smell, which was a mixture of post-mortem room, a sewer, sweat, and foul pus, for none of the windows were open, when I heard a scrabbling on the floor. I looked down in the half light, and saw a woman crouching at my feet. She had black matted hair, well populated, and her ribs stood out as though there were nothing between them, her arms were so thin that they were horrible. She was defecating, but she was so weak that she could not lift her buttocks from the floor, and as she had diarrhoea, the yellow liquid stools bubbled up over her thighs. Her feet were white and podgy from famine oedema, and she had scabies. As she crouched, she scratched her genital parts, which were scabetic too. Later on, we tried to pass a nasal tube on her, to give her protein hydrolysate, but her nose was so atrophied and blocked, that we could not get the thin tube down, and part of the nasal conchae came adrift on the end of it.

*[handwritten, vertical]: EXCESSIVE ACCUMULATION FLUID IN TISSUE*

*[handwritten, left margin]: WASTED AWAY*

*[handwritten]: HOLLOW PORTION*

But the floor was a minor consideration compared to the beds and the people. Most of the bunks had inmates, some two or three, and they were all smeared with faeces, because the people with diarrhoea did not bother to get out of bed. The result was that urine and faeces dribbled through the wooden boards of the top two bunks on to the lowest one, and as this last was the least comfortable, all the dying and weaker patients could be found there. Each patient had a collection of filthy tin cans and boxes at the head of their bed, where they stored their treasures and kept odd bits of

food. The worst cases had their hands covered with dried excreta, but it did not stop them eating or scratching. Some had no clothes at all, but the majority were dressed in blue and white striped night gowns. Outside, someone had dug a six-seater latrine, but the patients hardly used it at first, partly because they were too weak to walk the 30 feet to it, and partly because they were not used to that sort of luxury.

*Alan MacAuslan, medical student at St Thomas's Hospital Medical School*

**The ceremonial burning of the last hut on 21 May 1945. BU 6674**

*[handwritten, bottom]: SCABIES: CONTAGIOUS SKIN CONDITION CAUSED BY AN INSECT WHICH BURROWS UNDER LAYERS OF THE SKIN CAUSES GREAT ITCHING*

# STARVATION

Lack of food underlay most of the medical problems at Belsen. The inmates, weakened by hunger, and living in deteriorating sanitary conditions were more susceptible to diseases such as typhus, dysentery and enteritis. However, merely supplying food was not enough: the inmates could not tolerate the rich British army diet and many died when generosity by the soldiers outweighed caution. Special diets had to be formulated for the very sick and specialist nutrition teams from Britain's Medical Research Council and UNRRA were brought in to assist the army. Eventually the officers and men of the Royal Army Service Corps were providing five different diets to cope with the various levels of malnutrition.

*DYSENTERY = INFLAMMATION OF THE BOWELS*

*ENTERITIS = INFLAMMATION OF THE INTESTINAL TRACT.*

The outstanding deficiency was plain lack of food and water. More or less, malnutrition was evident in practically all patients: in some 60% it amounted to starvation.

*Lieutenant-Colonel F M Lipscomb FRCP RAMC, article in The Lancet, 8 September 1945*

Feeding the inmates was now the main priority. Anything else they'd either died from it already or were going to die from it very soon and one really couldn't do anything much about it.

*Ian Proctor, medical student at St Bartholomew's Hospital Medical School*

First of all the starving people had to be fed and in such a way that the sudden taking of food into their atrophied intestines did not itself cause intractable diarrhoea and death.

*Dr R A Collis, British Red Cross medical officer*

**A former prisoner, too weak to stand, attempts to drink soup provided by the British, 17 April 1945. BU 3752**

While we were evacuating the horror camp, my RSM had taken on the task of feeding some of the sick. There was little he could do, but by begging, borrowing and stealing food, he and eight men with him distributed 4,000 meals twice a day – a tremendous undertaking. The need of it was self-evident. The gunners were doing wonders in running a kitchen to which those internees who could walk would come with bins and collect food, hot soup etc, which they took back to the inmates of the huts where it was distributed. At least it got to those who were fit enough to come to the bins when they were brought to the huts. If they were too weak to go to the distributors or if they were of the wrong nationality, they got none. By the wrong nationality I mean that whatever nationality was in a majority in any hut they got the food. I believe there were exceptions, the Dutch and French would keep (*ie feed*) people of other races but in most cases there was a most distressing racial feeling.

*Lieutenant-Colonel M W Gonin, Commanding Officer 11 Light Field Ambulance, Royal Army Medical Corps*

Food distribution was a major problem, all the patients had an insatiable hunger and were invariably dissatisfied with the amounts they got: free fights between the different races were a common occurrence at meal times. Hoarding was almost universal and nearly every bed had mangled scraps of bread, butter etc hidden under the mattress or blanket.

*Major Hilda Roberts and Captain Petronella Potter, Queen Alexandra's Imperial Military Nursing Service*

The Bengal mixture was a mixture of dried milk, flour, sugar and molasses, an easily assimilable nourishment which we made up in huge, great vats to give to these people. It was very, no doubt, nutritious, but it was also very sickly and sweet. And I have a tremendous recollection of three Czechoslovakian Jewish doctors who were reasonably well preserved – they were very thin and emaciated but very much 'on the ball'. And they said to us, 'Look, it's all very well giving us this mixture, we are east Europeans and sweet food does not come nicely to us because we eat sour things and this sweet food is just revolting and what can you do?'...But sadly this Bengal mixture made them all sick and they rejected it. And I don't know, maybe we were trying to force too much food too quickly, I don't know – we were just

**Distribution of food to inmates of Belsen, 21 April 1945. These former prisoners look relatively healthy, which suggests that they had not been long in the camp. BU 4274**

dishing it out – but it certainly did not go down at all well. But there was nothing else so we gave out what we could.

We tried some intravenous nourishment – one or two brave chaps got hold of some intravenous transfusion sets from the nearby civilian hospital in the town of Celle. And this was desperate because they thought they were being done to death – you came in with a tube and a needle and they all thought they were just going to be slaughtered.

*John Dixey, medical student at St Bartholomew's Hospital Medical School*

Syringes were tricky things to wave around the place, as were stomach tubes as the SS seem to have had an unpleasant habit of injecting people with benzene to see what happened and the sight of a syringe caused hysterics in at least one of my patients.

*Alan MacAuslan, medical student at St Thomas's Hospital Medical School*

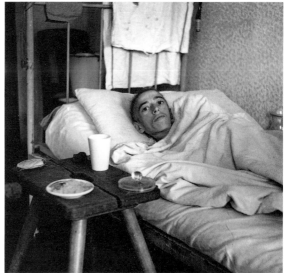

**Konrad Herschel, a fifteen-year-old Czech boy, in hospital at Belsen recoving from starvation. The photograph was taken on 20 July 1945, three months after the camp had been liberated. BU 9230**

# BURIAL OF THE DEAD

The ten thousand unburied corpses which lay throughout the camp remain one of the most appalling memories of Belsen. Prompt burial was essential to prevent further outbreaks of disease. The SS guards were made to bury the dead, but the task proved too much for them and eventually a bulldozer had to be used to push the bodies into mass graves. The absence of camp records meant that the exact number buried in the days immediately after liberation will never be known. It was only when the death rate had fallen to manageable proportions that accurate record keeping became possible. Services were read over the graves by Christian and Jewish chaplains. The photographs and film of the bulldozer at work remain among the most shocking images of the Second World War.

The bodies were a ghastly sight. Some were green. They looked like skeletons covered with skin – the flesh had all gone. There were bodies of small children among the grown ups. In other parts of the camp there were hundreds of bodies lying about, in many cases piled five or six high.

At another part of the camp our soldiers had started to organise the removal of piles of dead for burial. They had rounded up several SS men who were caught at the camp and had been there as guards. They were made to load lorries with bodies. They were kept on the move by our soldiers, picking up bodies from a heap and throwing them unceremoniously onto the trucks. The other inmates watched the loading, booing and shouting and throwing stones at the SS thugs. When the trucks were loaded the SS men were made to jump on top of the pile of bodies and the truck drove off to the burial place. On one of these trips one SS man jumped off and ran away. He only got a short distance before he was shot dead by a rain of bullets to the cheers of the crowd.

*Sergeant A N Midgley, No. 5 Army Film and Photographic Unit*

If it had been several hundred bodies one might have been really desperately upset and affected by it, mentally or psychologically at any rate. But no, it was on such a huge

**Unburied dead at Belsen. BU 3770**

SS guards forced to collect the dead for burial. BU 4025

SS guards throwing the bodies into one of the mass graves. BU 4060

scale, it was rather like trying to count the stars. There were thousands and thousands of dead bodies and you couldn't really relate to them as people, you couldn't really consider them to be your aunt or your mother or your brother or your father because there were just too many and they were being bulldozed into graves.

*John Dixey, medical student at St Bartholomew's Hospital Medical School*

The chap I felt sorry for mostly was a little chap in the engineers. He used to dig the holes out. Bulldozer. As soon as he'd finished one, he was about 12–14 feet down and then when he'd cleared it out he went to another site, started digging away there again. The officer was getting them to throw the bodies in because none of them had any identification on them no bracelets, no nothing, just throw 'em straight in. Then another officer came along and said, 'Look you're wasting your time doing that, put your bulldozer back on it.' So he was put in and this chap didn't like it at first. Then he started pushing them in and that's how it went on from there.

*Private Frederick Riches, 11 Light Field Ambulance, Royal Army Medical Corps*

British army chaplains read the burial service over one of the mass graves. BU 4267

**Burial of the dead using a bulldozer. This brutal method was used when it became clear that there were too many bodies to be individually collected. BU 4058**

# EVACUATION AND REHABILITATION

The decision to evacuate the camp was taken immediately after liberation: there could be no relief work amid the appalling conditions of the camp. As each hut was cleared it was burned, the last hut being ceremonially burned on 21 May. The evacuation of the camp marked the end of the first stage of the relief operation. The second stage was the rehabilitation, in mind and body, of the former inmates and their repatriation to their native lands. As the work progressed, tensions among the relief workers became evident. The inmates were not always easy to deal with and newcomers to Belsen did not always appreciate the difficulties which faced those who had worked there since April.

All patients would be taken from the Horror Camp completely naked and wrapped in blankets, they would go straight to what we called the Human Laundry where they would be washed, shaved and dusted by nurses from the German military hospital and then removed still naked to the wards in the hospital area.

*Lieutenant-Colonel M W Gonin, Commanding Officer 11 Light Field Ambulance, Royal Army Medical Corps*

Excitement at being selected for evacuation and the effort of getting in and out of the lorries and having a hot bath led to many collapses from exhaustion, so that it was necessary to establish a resuscitation point in the bath house. *No-one, having been selected, was left behind owing to the terrible depression and disappointment this would have caused.*

*Supplement to the* British Zone Review, *13 October 1945*

The MO went into each hut and marked on the forehead of each patient a cross to indicate to the bearers that this patient would be moved. The MO made no attempt to fix a diagnosis – all he did was decide whether the patient had any chance of living if he or she were moved or what the

Evacuation of the huts in Camp 1, 22 April 1945. Orderlies from 11 Light Field Ambulance, wearing protective clothing, remove a woman on a stretcher from one of the huts. BU 4195

chance of survival might be if the patient were left in the camp for another week. It was a heart-rending job and amounted to telling hundreds of poor wretches that they were being left to die.

*Lieutenant-Colonel M W Gonin, Commanding Officer 11 Light Field Ambulance, Royal Army Medical Corps*

The people that the officers had figured out, they was on one side of the hut, the others were being inspected over this side. The officers used to say, 'Take anybody you want from there.' We just went down, pointed out three people, out they come. There was no names, no nothing at all, just – we was sorry we couldn't get all of 'em out at once. They was all putting their hands up. 'I'm next! I'm next!' Some of them were even right at the back. They was shouting out, 'Take me! take me!' You went to the front and said, 'Right, you come out, you come out and you come out.' And that was it.

*Private Frederick Riches, 11 Light Field Ambulance, Royal Army Medical Corps*

**A woman pleads with an RAMC orderly for her children to be taken out of one of the huts. BU 4283**

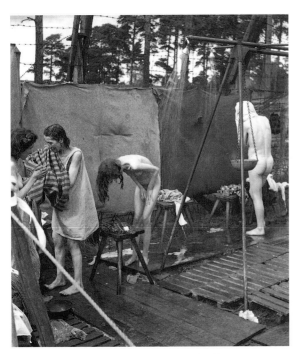

**Former inmates showering in one of the mobile cleansing sections before being transferred into accommodation in the nearby German barracks. BU 4237**

**Inside the 'Human Laundry', the stable block of the former Germany Army barracks. German nurses wash the body of an emaciated inmate, 1–4 May 1945. BU 5471**

I couldn't stand. I had no muscles, no flesh. Crawled on my knees.

'Out of here, out of this, here is only death, I must get out'.

Over the corpses, over the living, I don't remember who they were, out of the barrack, through the clay, it was very wet, yellow clay – out any direction. And then I remember it was sort of . . . I gave a gasp and I thought, 'I didn't make it' and I collapsed. But when I came to, I was lying there. Nobody picked me up, nobody had even seen me. One more, one less, didn't make any difference.

I looked around and where I had collapsed was actually the hut with the red cross on it. And when I'd got a little bit of strength – I crawled in through the door, the door was open and there was a long hall. On the left hand side behind the door was a pile of stretchers. About three. Couldn't have been very high. But for me in that state it was a sky-scraper. And I thought, 'What a pity it's so high. I could really, if I could pull myself a little bit up, I could really climb up and lie there for a little while.' But I couldn't make it. So I just sat down in the corner behind the door. Half of the door was closed where I was sitting, the other half was open . . .

I was very happy sitting there not knowing what comes next. The stretchers were here, next to me was the door and at least I was out of that block of death.

Middle of the night, suddenly the door opens, light is switched on and in front of me an English officer. Immediately he looked at me and he said in English, very, very severely, '*What are you doing here?*' And I was so pleased to see an Englishman instead of a German.

And the English came from that time when I was in the English Institute, and I smiled and I said, 'Nothing, I'm just sitting here', because that was exactly what I was doing. He used his official voice and said, '*What block do you belong to?*' – obviously under instructions to do the right thing. I said, 'Block number 11'. 'Well, I'm afraid you can't stay here because this is a Red Cross station. We are busy here. You have to go back and wait your turn'. More or less, 'you have to stay in the queue.' And I knew that is something I cannot do. I was a very obedient girl, always said 'yes', always was no trouble. But this was something else. This was my life and I knew.

**A view of one of the hospital blocks, clearly marked with the Red Cross, in the German barrack complex. BU 4707**

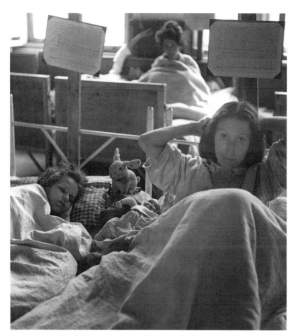

**A woman from Belsen, with her daughter by her side, lying in a clean bed in one of the newly created hospital blocks. BU 5481**

And I said, 'I'm sorry, I *cannot* go back and I will not go back because if I do, tomorrow I'll be dead and I know that.' And I said, 'You have been here now for a few days and you can see what you see, that life here is not worth that much – your nail on a little finger. But I tell you something: if you imagine somebody of your family in my place and you will leave me here, I will live and you will save one life.'

He looked and didn't say anything. And I said, 'Because if you think and want to make me go to Block 11, I would ask you to shoot me right here because I will not go.' He was standing there, listening, it went through his head and suddenly his face went like – you know, when you see in the films, when it starts swimming. It changed from this official military face where he observes rules into the human face who was underneath. I have no idea who he was. And he said, 'Right, you stay right here, don't let anybody touch you and I'll come and pick you up tomorrow morning.' . . . He picked me up like a little match, took me to another room where there was some kind of examination table, put me on top of the table and he said, 'Here you will lie and don't let anybody touch you, I will be here in the morning' and left.

After he had left I felt so dirty on that beautiful white table. I crawled down, lay on the floor and I thought, 'I've been lying on the floor for so long, one more night won't make any difference.' People were coming and going. Nobody paid any attention. Ten o'clock next morning, sure enough, he came. He came with a military truck – sort of Red Cross or ambulance car – where, when the doors were opened, there were four stretchers, two at the bottom, two at the top, all full. But he brought one extra and a sheet. He came, ripped off this memorable costume, threw it, kicked it, into the corner, wrapped me up in the sheet, strapped

me on the stretcher which was lying sort of in between the four – illegally* – closed the door and off we went.

And I remember when the car started to move I looked back. Sort of found enough strength to turn back. And through the slit of the back door I saw Belsen retreating and changing to the past. And I thought, 'After this, nothing but nothing can ever happen to me.'

And so he saved my life.

*Mrs Zdenka Ehrlich, Belsen inmate*

* The medical authorities tried, but without much success, to prevent the RAMC and RASC ambulance drivers from taking more than four inmates per ambulance for fear of overloading the facilities at the 'Human Laundry'.

The laundry consisted of a stable containing twenty tables which were staffed by forty German nurses and twenty German orderlies. A section of a mobile bath unit provided constant hot water. Patients were brought in at either end of the building, washed on the tables, dried and thoroughly covered with DDT powder. The cutting of hair was restricted to those whose heads were solid with lice. They were then placed in clean blankets and stretchers and transferred to hospital. In the course of twenty six days, 11,390 patients were dealt with in this manner. The average day's total was 650: the peak day was 970.

*Major E M Griffen RAMC and Major A P Prior RAMC*

Those girls (the German nurses) worked like slaves, they went down with typhus and they died but others took their place, they grew thin and they grew pale but they worked and they toiled from eight in the morning till six at night. They earned our respect.

*Lieutenant-Colonel M W Gonin, Commanding Officer 11 Light Field Ambulance, Royal Army Medical Corps*

**A former inmate in hospital being examined by medical staff both of whom were former Jewish internees: Dr Nysenhauz (left) and Sister Renée Erman (right). BU 4708**

Page from a sketch book drawn by fourteen-year-old Hannah Sachsel while in hospital at Belsen.
HU 59502B, Andrew Matthews Collection

This sounds quite a simple procedure, but believe me, it is far from it. I could not attempt to explain the difficulties. The chief one is that of languages. The majority of patients have some Jewish origin but are from all countries under the sun: Russia, Poland, Hungary, Czechoslovakia, Belgium, Holland, France and about a few of them have a smattering of English.

*Sister Kathleen Elvidge, QAIMNS, 29 British General Hospital*

The ward was light and airy with an atmosphere of hope. There were vases of fresh flowers on the table and an ancient radio blared out music from the American Forces Network whenever the two army orderlies could make it work. Corporal Alexander was a large Scot who had the knack of acquiring everything we needed plus a few extra luxuries for the patients after his occasional sorties into the village with his Sten gun and a good vocabulary of international four letter words!

His presents were the tonic needed to humanize the women again. Despite few common languages, there was laughter and happiness as the make-up and hair-dos transformed them back to normality. Deaths were no longer treated with indifference, in fact, the two that occurred during my stay were more like family bereavements, even though there were no families present.

One morning there was great excitement on the ward when Hannah Sachsel started her first period. She was fourteen and had managed to survive with her seventeen-year-old sister Eva. Everybody loved them as they symbolised the immortality of youth and hope. It was celebrated like a miracle as no-one had menstruated since entering the camp.

*Andrew Matthews, medical student at St Mary's Hospital Medical School*

They (*the inmates*) are making an infernal mess of this camp, and all their destruction is so wanton as they destroy anything which is of no use to them at the present moment irrespective of the fact that they might want it later, and they still live by the ' law of the clutching hand.'

Some Army nursing sisters and a Major from 29 British General Hospital had just arrived and there were several blow-ups between the nursing sisters and our chaps – the sisters tried to order them around in their own wards and as we were still in charge they were told, none too politely, where to get off.

Rehabilitation: Irene Mandel, a former internee, teaches at the school set up by the Jewish committee at Belsen. BU 7802

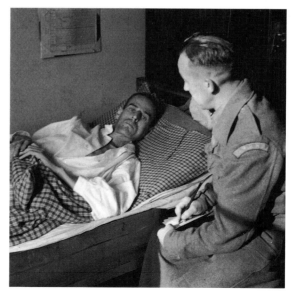

An UNRRA official interviews a former inmate to arrange his repatriation to Poland. BU 9224

Then the Matron went round and started to criticise our hospital and another chap blew up at her. It was a great pity that these people had not seen the conditions in Camp 1 and compare them with the Roundhouse. Tempers were beginning to run pretty high.

*Michael Hargrave, student at Westminster Hospital Medical School*

**Distribution of clothing to former internees before their journey home. Vivian Dantell, an UNRRA worker, helps Livia Crammer select a pair of shoes, 16–17 May 1945. BU 6366**

The horror camp was completely destroyed by fire. That was the only possible end to a place which had seen so much human misery, degradation and horror.

*Lieutenant-Colonel J A D Johnstone, Commanding Officer 32 Casualty Clearing Station, Royal Army Medical Corps*

I could write a paean of praise to the teachers and supervisors of the schools, for it is their goal to bring normalcy into the lives of the children, to do everything possible to make them forget the horrors and travails of the preceding years.

*Vida Kaufman, American relief worker*

Let us not forget too, the great humanitarian service rendered us by Count Bernadotte's Swedish Red Cross. This is a glorious unselfish story of human sacrifice – some 6,000 very sick people were taken from Belsen for treatment in Swedish hospitals.

*Josef Rosensaft, Chairman of the Jewish Central Committee at Belsen*

Malmo, 22 July 1945

My dear Andrew,

I think you will be very astonished to get a letter from Sweden. A week ago we arrived here. We are in a quarantine for three weeks but after these three weeks we are free. Andrew, I am the happiest person in the world, I have found my brother here in Sweden. After seven years I have seen him again, he looks very well. After the quarantine I am going to him, I think I will have a good time. We have not much money but we are so happy you can't imagine.

*Extract from a letter written to Andrew Matthews, a medical student from St Mary's Hospital, by Lisl Schmidt, a Czech inmate of Belsen who was one of 6,000 Belsen inmates evacuated by the Red Cross to Sweden*

**Former Belsen inmates are taken on board the Swedish Red Cross ship *Ronnskar* in July 1945. Six thousand Belsen inmates were taken to Sweden for treatment. BU 9225**

# THE BELSEN TRIAL

The trial of Josef Kramer and forty four other Belsen guards was held at Luneburg between 17 September and 17 November 1945 and was the first war crimes trial to be held by the Allies. The defendants were charged with having been responsible for the ill-treatment and death of prisoners at Auschwitz, where Kramer had been the Kommandant of the Birkenau extermination complex and many other Belsen guards had previously been stationed, and at Belsen. Each of the accused was defended by a British barrister. On 17 November Kramer and ten others were sentenced to death by hanging and twenty others to varying terms of imprisonment. The remaining fourteen defendants were acquitted. The death sentences were carried out at Hamelin Gaol on 12 December after the condemned had had their appeals for clemency rejected.

May it please the Court. Each of the charges in this case are that when the accused were members of the staff of one or other of these two concentration camps, and as such responsible for the well-being of the prisoners interned there, in violation of the law and usages of war they were together concerned as parties to the ill-treatment of certain of the persons interned in the camp, and by that ill-treatment they caused the death of some and they caused physical suffering to others.

*Lieutenant-Colonel T M Backhouse, Counsel for the Prosecution, opening address to the Court, 17 September 1945*

Q. Subsequently did you go to Belsen?

A. On 18 January I arrived at Belsen and was put into Block 28. The conditions were so bad that it is impossible to find words in this world. In half a barracks there were 600 to 700 people. We were lying on the floor covered with lice and every other kind of vermin one could imagine. Our food depended very largely on the efforts of the senior of the block. If she was energetic we might get a quarter basin of soup at midday, if not, we might get it at three o'clock. There was no bread for four weeks before the arrival of the British troops. During the whole time I was at Belsen, people were not taken for baths nor were their clothes changed. Towards morning there were several hundred corpses in the blocks and around the blocks.

*Dora Szafran, inmate at Belsen and witness for the prosecution. Evidence given on 24 September 1945*

**The scene inside the courtroom at Luneberg during the Belsen Trial showing the accused sitting in the dock. HU 59545**

Q. Is not the truth of the matter that you never tried in any way to help these people at all?

A. That is not true. I had written to several firms to get additional food.

Q. I suggest that the transports poured in for precisely the same reason they poured into Birkenau.

A. No.

Q. I suggest that you never even troubled to clear up the corpses until you knew a truce was being signed.

A. If that was true I could have spared many litres of diesel oil. Only five days before the arrival of British troops the corpses were taken to the crematorium by truck and horse-drawn cart.

Q. Do you know how many thousands were lying unburied in the camp when the British came?

A. No. It was reported to me by the *Lagerführer* two days before the British came that there were no more corpses lying about in the men's compound.

Q. Do you know that the British found 13,000 corpses lying unburied in that camp?

A. I cannot believe it.

*Cross-examination of Josef Kramer by Lieutenant-Colonel T M Backhouse, Counsel for the Prosecution, 9 October 1945*

I say that Kramer was responsible for the conditions, among other reasons, because on one occasion when I complained of the increasing death rate to Kramer he replied, 'Let them die, why should you care?'

I remember an occasion at Belsen some time in February or March when an escaped prisoner, either a Polish or a German woman, was caught after trying to escape. Kramer, the Kommandant, questioned the girl in front of several of us SS women and I saw him kicking and shaking her and later hit her with a stick on her head and face and all over her body quite unmercifully.

*Deposition of Hilda Ehlert, former Aufseherin (wardress) at Belsen*

Q. With regard to the Russian girl who escaped and whose ears you say you boxed, Ehlert stated that she saw you kicking and shaking her and later hitting her with a stick on her head and face and all over her body quite unmercifully.

A. I told you already that I slapped her face. I did not have a stick in my hand.

Q. Ehlert says that as a result the girl gave the names of two girls whom she said had helped her to escape, that you sent for these two girls and gave instructions for each of them to receive five strokes on the bare behind to make them confess.

A. No, I never issued such an order either in Birkenau or Belsen.

Q. I suggest to you that you beat that girl, that you know you did and that that answer is no more truthful than any of the other answers you have given this afternoon.

A. I have said nothing but the truth.

*Cross-examination of Josef Kramer by Lieutenant-Colonel T M Backhouse, Counsel for the Prosecution, 9 October 1945*

Finally in the last, Kramer stood completely deserted by his superiors, while these waves of circumstances beat around him. Since the date of liberation by the British, Josef Kramer, former Kommandant, has been brandished throughout the world as 'The Beast of Belsen'. When the curtain finally rings down on this stage Josef Kramer will, in my submission, stand forth not as the 'The Beast of Belsen' but as 'The Scapegoat of Belsen', the scapegoat for the man Heinrich Himmler, whose bones are rotting on Luneburg Heath not very far from here, and the scapegoat for the whole National Socialist system.

*Major T C M Winwood RA, defending officer for Josef Kramer, 8 October 1945*

No-one will ever persuade me that the camp staff were the helpless victims of circumstances that they made out they were at the recent Belsen trials.

*Lieutenant-Colonel M W Gonin, Commanding Officer, 11 Light Field Ambulance, Royal Army Medical Corps*

**Major-General H P Berney-Ficklin, President of the British Military Court. HU 59546**

**SS wardress Irma Grese, who along with Kommandant Kramer and nine other Belsen guards was hanged on 12 December 1945. BU 9700**

On further reflection I wish to say that in three respects the statements I made in my previous deposition were not accurate. First of all I stated that I never carried arms. In fact *Aufseherinnen* at Auschwitz did carry pistols, I among them. My pistol, however, was never loaded and I did not know how to use it nor did I ever do so. Second, when I stated that the only time I used a weapon to beat prisoners was when I had a whip for a week: this was untrue. I did, in fact, always have a whip which I used consistently whenever necessary. Third, I admit there was a walking stick which we kept in the *Lageraltester*'s room and which, although it was unauthorised, we frequently used to beat prisoners. I

usually used to beat them on the shoulders, but there were times when, because of the numbers involved, they were beaten on any part of the body that happened to be easiest. All the beatings to which I refer were immediate and I have never taken part in deliberately organised punishments. If it was desired to inflict an organised beating the prisoner had to be reported and confined to a special cell pending punishment. I never saw any such punishment carried out.

*Third and final deposition of Irma Grese,* Aufseherin *(wardress) at Auschwitz and Belsen*

Have you any doubt at all that Kramer was right in it at Belsen? Ehlert said that he had told her, 'Let them die, why should you care.' You have heard what Klein (*camp doctor*) said about it: 'I am not taking orders from you.' You have heard that his attitude when Brigadier Glyn Hughes and Colonel Johnston arrived was absolutely callous to the whole thing. You have the individual beatings he has given in Belsen. Sunschein (*prosecution witness*) said that the whole block was made to kneel in the rain and deprived of food for 24 hours by him because some Russian girls had stolen bread. There is the story by Bimko and Hammermasch (*prosecution witnesses*) of him beating a Russian, who was building a shelter, until he was unconscious, and kicking him on the ground.

This Court is doing justice, and if you have any reasonable doubt in the case of any of the accused, quite rightly you will acquit them. If, on the other hand, you are satisfied in respect of all or any of these persons that they knew what was happening, that they realized that these people were dying of neglect, and they took part in it, then, in my submission, there can be only one verdict on whichever charge it may be, and that is that they are guilty. This case started, by a singular coincidence, on the Jewish Day of Atonement. It is a very long time ago, and if the Court are satisfied of the guilt of any of these prisoners then they have only one duty, and that is to declare them guilty.

*Lieutenant-Colonel T M Backhouse, Counsel for the Prosecution, concluding address to the Court, 13 November 1945*

# REFLECTIONS

I was anxious to take the opportunity of seeing with my own eyes. If in five years time I hear people saying that Belsen etc, were so much propaganda, I shall be in a position to argue from conviction.

*Squadron Leader F J Lyons, HQ 8501 Wing, Royal Air Force*

Belsen was an experience no-one could ever forget. Everyone who was there must have acquired a greater understanding and appreciation of tolerance and service to others. Not one of us who was not a prisoner there can ever realise what those brave people went through and endured.

*Brigadier H L Glyn-Hughes, Deputy Director of Medical Services Second Army*

The work of the doctors and nurses who came to us from the British Army will for ever remain a ray of sunlight in those dark and tragic days. They may have the satisfaction of knowing that those who recovered are everlastingly grateful for the human service rendered them so generously.

*Dr Hadassah Bimko, internee doctor*

This letter will read like fiction and will seem to be an exaggeration but I swear that as sure as there is a God in heaven that what I have told you is the Gospel truth.

*Gunner George Walker, 113 Light Anti-Aircraft Regiment, Royal Artillery*

The world has heard a good deal of the horrors of Belsen – it has heard all too little of the gallantry of the handful of men and women, the staff of a field ambulance, a casualty clearing station and a mobile laboratory, who had the courage to tackle one of the most terrible and immense medical problems that has ever arisen.

*Dr (later Dame) Janet Vaughan, Medical Research Council team leader at Belsen*

There are no wreaths or flowers in our hands as we stand before you, our dearly beloved and hallowed dead, to bid farewell to you, without ceremony and celebration, as we leave the spot in which are buried the stubs and embers of your sacred Jewish bodies, we whisper and sign our Shalom as we depart never to return.

*Josef Rosensaft, Chairman of the Jewish Central Committee at Belsen. Eulogy on the closing of Belsen camp, 6 September 1950*

It was only when I got back to Britain and saw three empty tables in our operating theatre, and people walking round our streets, knowing that they had homes to go to and families that had not been burnt alive, that the horror of it all dawned on me.

*Alan MacAuslan, medical student at St Thomas's Hospital Medical School*

# RELIEF OF BELSEN: UNITS INVOLVED

The following is a list of units of the Second Army which were formally allocated to relief work in Belsen. However, during the course of the operation many other units from Second Army were called upon to provide assistance on a temporary basis.

## Royal Artillery
63 Anti-Tank Regiment
113 Light Anti-Aircraft Regiment

## Royal Army Medical Corps, Royal Army Dental Corps and Queen Alexandra's Imperial Military Nursing Service
11 Light Field Ambulance
163 Field Ambulance
32 Casualty Clearing Station
35 Casualty Clearing Station
9 British General Hospital
29 British General Hospital
30 Field Hygiene Section
76 Field Hygiene Section
  Field Transfusion Unit
22 Field Transfusion Unit
30 Field Transfusion Unit
! Vascular Injuries Research Team
7 Mobile Bacteriological Laboratory

## United States Army Medical Corps
US Army Typhus Commission

## Royal Army Service Corps
1575 Artillery Platoon (Light)
1576 Artillery Platoon (Heavy)
155 Detail Issue Depot
102 Mobile Laundry and Bath Unit
D Platoon, 567 Company, RASC (American Field Service)

## Royal Engineers
612 Field Squadron

## Royal Electrical and Mechanical Engineers
113 Workshops

## Military Government
10 Garrison Detachment
102 Control Section
224 Detachment
618 Detachment
904 Detachment
912 Detachment
12 Displaced Persons Assembly Team
3 Military Government Inland Detachment
Judge Advocate General War Crimes Commission

## Miscellaneous
Army Chaplains Department
35 Pioneer Group, Royal Pioneer Corps
14 Amplifier Unit, Intelligence Corps
No.5 Army Film and Photographic Unit
Deputy Assistant Director Ordnance Services Dump
Fire and Water Group HQ

## Volunteer Organisations
103, 104, 105, 113, 114 British Red Cross & Order of St John's Ambulance Sections
Detachments of the Swiss and Swedish Red Cross
Vatican Relief Team
Team RS100 of the Friends' (Quaker) Relief Service
UNRRA Relief Team
Medical Research Council Relief Team
British medical students from the London teaching hospitals
Belgian medical students

# BIBLIOGRAPHY

M Caiger-Smith, (Ed), *The Face of the Enemy: British Photographers in Germany, 1944–45*, Dirk Nishen Publishing, 1988.

F A E Crew, *Medical History of the Second World War: Army Medical Services, Campaigns Vol IV, North West Europe*, HMSO, London, 1962.

F S V Donnison, *Civil Affairs and Military Government in North West Europe 1944–46*, HMSO, London, 1961.

Konilyn Feig, *Hitler's Death Camps*, Holmes and Meier Publishers Inc., New York, 1979.

Paul Kemp, 'The Relief of Belsen, April 1945: the testimony of those involved', *Imperial War Museum Review No. 5*, Imperial War Museum, London, 1990.

Eberhard Kolb, *Bergen-Belsen: Geschichte des Aufenthaltslagers 1943–45*, Verlag fur Literatur und Zeitgeschehen, Hannover, 1962.

Eberhard Kolb, *Bergen-Belsen: From Detention Camp to Concentration Camp*, Niedersachsische Landeszentrale fur Politische Bildung, Sammlung Vandenhoeck, 1985.

H Leiviek, et al, *Belsen*, Irgun Sheerit Hapleita Me'haezor Habriti, Tel Aviv, 1957.

Brenda McBride, *Quiet Heroines: Nurses of the Second World War*, Chatto and Windus, London, 1985.

R McLaughlin, *The Royal Army Medical Corps*, Leo Cooper, 1972.

Juliet Piggott, *Queen Alexandra's Royal Army Nursing Corps*, Leo Cooper, London, 1975.

## Note on sources held at the Imperial War Museum

**Department of Photographs**: holds approximately 500 Photographs taken by members of No.5 Army Film and Photographic Unit (AFPU). The bulk of the material concentrates on the condition of the camp when liberated by the British Army and the early stages of the relief operation. A separate series of Agency photographs covers the Belsen trial.

**Department of Film**: holds a considerable amount of unedited, mute, black and white film taken by cameramen in No.5 AFPU. The content of the film is very similar to that of the photographs. There are also a number of contemporary newsreel films.

**Department of Documents**: responsible for keeping private papers of those involved in the liberation. The most important collection is a paper written by **Lieutenant-Colonel M W Gonin DSO RAMC**, Commanding Officer of 11 Light Field Ambulance, one of the first medical units to enter Belsen. Other collections of note are diaries kept by **David Bradford** and **Michael Hargrave**, two of the medical student volunteers; a letter and a medical notebook kept by **Michael Coigley**, another of the medical students; and a letter from **Sergeant A N Midgley**, one of the photographers in No.5 AFPU. The Department also holds the papers of **Major T C M Winwood** who was Kramer's defending officer at the Belsen trial. Other collections held by the Department of Documents include those of **Sister Kathleen Elvidge, Brigadier R H T Daniell DSO, Squadron Leader F J Lyons** and **Gunner George Walker**.

**Department of Sound Records**: has extensive interviews with former inmates of Belsen and those involved in the liberation. Quoted in this booklet are the reminiscences of **Mrs Zdenka Ehrlich, Private Frederick Riches, John Roger Dixey, David Bradford** and **I R Proctor**.

Further details about the Museum's collections may be obtained by writing to the appropriate Department.